Easy Spanish Phrases for Kids

CHILDREN'S LEARN SPANISH BOOKS

BABY PROFESSOR

EDUCATION KIDS

Speedy Publishing LLC

40 E. Main St. #1156

Newark, DE 19711

www.speedypublishing.com

Copyright 2016

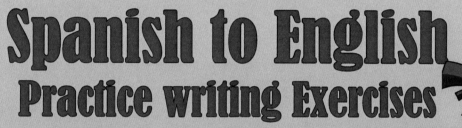

Spanish to English
Practice writing Exercises

Trace and rewrite the spanish phrases
and english translations.

¿hablas español?

Ponte los zapatos.

Ponte los zapatos.

Put on your shoes.

Put on your shoes.

Cepíllate los dientes.

Cepíllate los dientes.

Brush your teeth.

Brush your teeth.

Do you speak spanish?

Que descanses.

Que descanses.

Sleep well. (Sleep tight.)

Sleep well. (Sleep tight.)

Que sueñes con los angelitos.

Que sueñes con los angelitos.

Sweet dreams.

Sweet dreams.

¿hablas español?

Te adoro.

Te adoro.

I love you (I adore you).

I love you (I adore you).

Te quiero.

Te quiero.

I love you.

I love you.

Do you speak spanish?

¿Quieres agua?
Español

¿Quieres agua?

Do you want some water?
English translation

Do you want some water?

Lávate las manos
Español

Lávate las manos

Wash your hands.
English translation

Wash your hands.

¿hablas español?

Toma mi mano.

Toma mi mano.

Take my hand.

Take my hand.

Dame un abrazo.

Dame un abrazo.

Give me a hug.

Give me a hug.

Do you speak spanish?

Siéntate.

Siéntate.

Sit down.

Sit down.

Muy calladito/a por favor

Muy calladito/a por favor

Be really quiet.

Be really quiet.

¿hablas español?

Ven acá.

Ven acá.

Come here.

Come here.

No toques.

No toques.

Don't touch.

Don't touch.

Do you speak spanish?

Camina, por favor.

Camina, por favor.

Walk, please.

Walk, please.

No corras.

No corras.

Don't run.

Don't run.

¿hablas español?

Amárrate los zapatos

Amárrate los zapatos

Tie your shoes.

Tie your shoes.

Dime otra vez.

Dime otra vez.

Tell me again.

Tell me again.

Do you speak spanish?

Hazlo de nuevo

Español

Hazlo de nuevo

Do it again.

English translation

Do it again.

¿Quieres leer?

Español

¿Quieres leer?

Do you want to read a story?

English translation

Do you want to read a story?

¿hablas español?

¿Cuántos hay?

¿Cuántos hay?

How many are there?

How many are there?

¡Mira!

¡Mira!

Look.

Look.

Do you speak spanish?

Buenos días
Español

Buenos días

Good morning
English translation

Good morning

¿Cómo amaneciste?
Español

¿Cómo amaneciste?

How are you this morning?
English translation

How are you this morning?

¿hablas español?

Tenemos que irnos en....minutos

Tenemos que irnos en....minutos

We have to go in ... minutes

We have to go in ... minutes

Tiende la cama.

Tiende la cama.

Make your bed.

Make your bed.

Do you speak spanish?

¿Te gusta?

¿Te gusta?

Do you like it?

Do you like it?

Me toca.

Me toca.

It's my turn.

It's my turn.

¿hablas español?

Te toca.

Te toca.

It's your turn.

It's your turn.

Cierra la puerta.

Cierra la puerta.

Close the door.

Close the door.

Do you speak spanish?

Apágalo.

Español

Apágalo.

Turn it off.

English translation

Turn it off.

Pon la mesa

Español

Pon la mesa

Set the table.

English translation

Set the table.

¿hablas español?

Ayúdame, por favor.

Ayúdame, por favor.

Help me please.

Help me please.

¿Te ayudo?

¿Te ayudo?

Can I help you?

Can I help you?

Do you speak spanish?

Por favor

Por favor

Please

Please

Gracias

Gracias

Thank you

Thank you

¿hablas español?

Bien hecho.

Bien hecho.

Well done.

Well done.

Intenta otra vez.

Intenta otra vez.

Try again.

Try again.

Do you speak spanish?

De nada

Español

De nada

You're welcome.

English translation

You're welcome.

Con cuidado / Ten cuidado

Español

Con cuidado / Ten cuidado

Be careful.

English translation

Be careful.

¿hablas español?

Guarda los juguetes

Guarda los juguetes

Pick up your toys.

Pick up your toys.

¿Acabaste?

¿Acabaste?

Are you done?

Are you done?

Do you speak spanish?

A la cama

A la cama

Time for bed.

Time for bed.

Apaga la luz.

Apaga la luz.

Turn off the light.

Turn off the light.

¿hablas español?

¿Dónde estás?

¿Dónde estás?

Where are you?

Where are you?

Ganaste.

Ganaste.

You won.

You won.

Do you speak spanish?

Gané.

Gané.

I won.

I won.

Dame la mano.

Dame la mano.

Give me your hand.

Give me your hand.

¿hablas español?

Me encanta.

Me encanta.

I love it.

I love it.

Lo haces bien.

Lo haces bien.

You do that well.

You do that well.

Do you speak spanish?

Lo hiciste bien.

Lo hiciste bien.

You did it really well.

You did it really well.

Me gusta

Me gusta

I like it.

I like it.

¿hablas español?

Es hora de dormir.

Es hora de dormir.

It's time to go to sleep.

It's time to go to sleep.

Es hora de ir a la cama.

Es hora de ir a la cama.

It's time for bed.

It's time for bed.

Do you speak spanish?

Buenas noches

Buenas noches

Good night

Good night

¿Tienes hambre?

¿Tienes hambre?

Are you hungry?

Are you hungry?

¿hablas español?

A comer

A comer

Come eat.

Come eat.

Es hora de comer

Es hora de comer

It's time to eat.

Are you hungry?

Do you speak spanish?

Come.

Español

Come.

Eat.

English translation

Eat.

Cómetelo

Español

Cómetelo

Eat it up.

English translation

Are you hungry?

¿hablas español?

¿Quieres más?

¿Quieres más?

Do you want more?

Do you want more?

Estoy tan contento

Estoy tan contento

I'm so glad

I'm so glad

Do you speak spanish?

Me comí el chocolate

Español

Me comí el chocolate

I ate the chocolate

English translation

I ate the chocolate

Me encanta dibujar

Español

Me encanta dibujar

I love to draw

English translation

I love to draw

¿hablas español?

Me haces feliz

Español

Me haces feliz

You make me happy

English translation

You make me happy

Mi primer amor

Español

Mi primer amor

My first love

English translation

My first love

Do you speak spanish?

Muchos te amo

Muchos te amo

I love you very much

I love you very much

No puedo vivir sin ti

No puedo vivir sin ti

I can't live without you

I can't live without you

¿hablas español?

Pienso en ti siempre

Español

Pienso en ti siempre

I always think of you

English translation

I always think of you

Jugar basketball

Español

Jugar basketball

Play basketball

English translation

Play basketball

Do you speak spanish?

Puedo color?

Puedo color?

Can I color it?

Can I color it?

Hola Maestro!

Hola Maestro!

Hi Teacher!

Hi Teacher!